The Green Man

The Green Man

David Russell Mosley

RESOURCE *Publications* • Eugene, Oregon

THE GREEN MAN

Resource Publications
An Imprint of Wipf and Stock Publishers
199 W. 8th Ave., Suite 3
Eugene, OR 97401

www.wipfandstock.com

PAPERBACK ISBN: 978-1-6667-0367-2
HARDCOVER ISBN: 978-1-6667-0368-9
EBOOK ISBN: 978-1-6667-0369-6

MAY 10, 2021

Many of these poems first appeared in *The Imaginative Conservative*, *Jesus the Imagination*, *Macrina Magazine*, and *Z Publishing*.

To Southwell Minster whose beautiful architecture first introduced me to the Green Man.

The poet's eye, in fine frenzy rolling,

Doth glance from heaven to earth, from earth to heaven;

And as imagination bodies forth

The forms of things unknown, the poet's pen

Turns them to shapes and gives to airy nothing

A local habitation and a name.

> —THESEUS,
> *A Midsummer Night's Dream*, Act V Scene I

Contents

Preface

In some ways, it would be correct to say that this collection of poetry began with a tour through Southwell Minster in England in 2012. A group of friends and I had come out to visit theologians John and Alison Milbank. John decided to take us on a walking tour of the village, including a walk through the minster. While, like most church buildings in the UK, much of the current building dates back to the 18th century, the chapter house dates from the 10th or 11th. The buildings are beautiful, filled with stone-cut leaves, but also with these foliate heads, which many now call the Green Man.

I became fascinated with this local, architectural figure who had hints of various folkloric elements about him, and yet could not be simply taken back to any one of them. Six years later, I begin writing poetry in earnest. Thanks to the encouragement of friends, I begin to think that perhaps I have some meager skill in the making of verse. I write poems about everything, but one figure who keeps creeping into them is the enigmatic Green Man. And so this volume exists.

The poems in this volume are divided into seven sections. The first is a collection of poems contemplating the days of creation, thinking about the original goodness and impending disaster. Then a few poems deal with the fall, this loss of sight. For that is what I think the Green Man represents in many ways; he represents a truer vision of reality, a better relationship with God's creation. The next four sections look to the four seasons. Most of these poems could broadly be considered nature poems, but there are others about home life, the seemingly ordinary. Poetry helps us see that the "ordinary" is anything but. It forces us to see things in a new light. And that is what I have tried to do in these poems.

The final section deals with saints and other holy ideas. I focus primarily on saints and stories related to nature. Here you will meet St. Patrick, St. Brigid, St. Francis, and others. These figures represent for me the kind of relationship we are supposed to have with creation.

In all of these poems I have tried to get at something which our senses have forgotten how to sense. I use meter and rhyme and metaphor to help break us out of what Coleridge called the "film of familiarity." We have lost many things in our fall from grace. But perhaps if we pay closer attention, then by the grace of God, we can see them anew, see them as we ought to see them.

David Russell Mosley
Spokane
Christmas Eve, 2020

Acknowledgements

So many have helped me on the way to this, my first poetry collection. I must first thank my good friend, Mark Forrester, who heard the majority of these poems in their very first drafts. His encouragement directly led to the publication of this book. Then there is The Group Who Was Thursday, a small gathering of writers living in Southern New Hampshire which Mark and I helped found. Their support and criticism helped bring these poems to life. I'd like to specially thank Elizabeth Pope, Julia Kaschak, and Derek McDonald for their work in reading through the book for misplaced punctuation. Next, I'd like to thank Anne Michelle Carpenter and Sally Thomas. These two excellent poets helped me clarify my language and gave me encouragement to keep writing. I also want to thank Malcolm Guite, the poet, theologian, rock-star, who showed me that formal poetry can still have legs and still bring meaning in this modern age. Lastly, and most importantly, I wish to thank my wife Lauren. Without her love and constant support, I would not be the man I am today and thus would not be the poet I am today.

Woodcut by Tyler DeLong

Creation

"In the Beginning"

In the beginning, the cosmos unfurls and lights
The darkness of nothingness: a symphony.
In the beginning, God speaks, delights
In us, and speaks himself in harmony.
In the beginning, waters turn and toss.
The Spirit hovers in ordering love and laughs.
In the beginning, that nothingness we call chaos
Receives the stamp of form as the Word chants.
In the beginning, Form receives its shape,
The Image shapes all things unto himself.
In the beginning microcosmic atoms traipse
About the expanse, pictures of the cosmic wealth.
In the beginning, time begins its joyful song,
And when it began we knew how to sing along.

"Day One"

What is this Light spoken into being,
The one which separates Day from Night?
Before the sun and other stars, it brings
Meaning to the Cosmos. It is the Light
Of the Unending first Day. It radiates
Out into Wisdom, time, and space, continual
Creation. It sets the world ablaze, conflagrates
The dark, illuminates the night, noumenal
Glory. It is before phenomena,
And once we were bathed in it, this light maternal.
It suffused the earth, the prolegomenon.
But now we do not see this light eternal,
We looked in for its source, and missed it there.
Perhaps we still know how to look, but where?

"The Second Day"

What does it mean, he made a dome, a wall
To separate the waters below from those
Above? What are these waters above it all,
This cosmic ocean beyond the heavens? He chose
Mystery to describe to us the canvas
Of the night and day. And just what is the sky?
The abode of gods, of angels, of stars and planets?
Of clouds, of airish wights, where beanstalks high
Reach up to the homes of giants awaiting their end?
It is unfilled potential, beautiful
Potency, which to our imagination bends,
But only after the unfilled becomes full.
His "Let there be," creates the space for more.
He sees it good and good it is therefore.

"The Third Day"

The seas subside, drawing back to unveil the land.
From light and dark you move to earth and water.
You multiply by adding through division,
Order to chaos and back to order after.
Then bursting up from underneath the earth,
Trees and shrubs and bushes and plants grow tall.
The trees dig deep and spread their roots further,
But the forests do not stay on land, but go over all
The globe, and under the sea and everywhere.
From void to light and dark, a water dome
To separate the earth and sky, another
Separation creates for us a home,
Because you begin by making space to fill,
Preparing for those to whom you'll give free will.

"The Fourth Day"

The celestial lights were spoken into being,
One to govern day, the other night.
They give to us the happy gift of seeing,
And shape to the day on which he made the Light.
He set the shining orbs to mark the seasons,
Of when to plow and when to rest in peace,
But they also give us hints as to the reason
God's Light must be mediated through grace.
They also serve as symbols and as signs,
"The Heavens declare the Glory of the Lord,"
And we look to them just as the Lover pines
After the Beloved's lingering, loving words.
And so he set them as guides and not as bars
To teach us, and he also made the stars.

"The Fifth Day"

The birds all fly their pelicanic flights,
Prepared to pierce their hearts to feed their young.
The phoenix on its pyre-like nest alights
And burns, the song that never goes unsung.
You made the birds to fill the ancient air,
The aves sing *Ave* to the morning sun.
But in the deeps, leviathan has his lair,
And swam before on land a man could run.
The spirits of the air and seas receive
These gifts from you on their creation day
To care for them and guide us to believe
That you made the world in which we live and play.
For still the world was not yet wholly filled.
It waited yet for creatures with free will.

"The Sixth Day"

The lumbering beasts all graze upon the land,
And offer up themselves to one another.
Not just survival but harmony and
Symbiosis was how the world was governed.
This is the garden into which we were born,
When from the dust our shapes received a soul.
We were set as farmers at the dawn,
But in two nights we would stumble and fall.
Still, until then we wandered round the world,
Caring for each creature as our brother,
Sister, the earth as Mother, now curled
Up in this heavenly home as lovers.
We did not know just then that we would sin,
So we journeyed further upward, further in.

"The Seventh Day"

You left the final day for re-creation,
For art and song and festive feasts for all.
You knew we'd work and toil to our damnation,
So you left us space where we could wholly call
Upon your name. Our feasts and songs are sourced
In celebration of you, our only Lord.
You gave us life and yet we were not forced
To listen to your voice, your holy Word.
And when we fell, you did not take the space
You set aside to give us rest and play.
Instead you came and took from death our place,
So from the night we could find the final day.
The week is done, but soon that day is coming,
When we at last will have eternal Sonning.

Loss

"The Fall"

Our ancient ancestors once thought
The world was wreathed in fire, sublunary.
It sat at the bottom, unimportant, cosmically
Speaking. It was rife with change and fraught
With sin. Beneath the moon we lived and fought.
We saw the stars shining eternally,
And longed for more from the Translunary.
We hoped, we prayed, we longed for we knew not what.
Then the Light came down, no refracted light,
But mediated through our very self.
He crossed the divide we could not cross on our own.
He came to separate and to unite,
Man from man and man unto himself.
He united us all and came to bring us home.

But we are divided one from another,
From brother sun and too from brother fire,
From sister moon and from the Earth our mother,
From brook and sea, from tree and branch and briar.
And from the fox and deer and bear and dove
We are sundered. We pillage and rape,
Destroying fox's den and the foxgloves.
We leave them nowhere to hide, nowhere to escape.
But who do we hate more, the world or ourselves?
We seem to live as if we were all rocks,
Isolated and alone, the bells
Of warning, ringing out the awes and shocks.
Yet one came into this destructive pile,
The one in whom there is neither Jew nor gentile.

Yet how can I learn to love the Other

When I am sundered from my own self?
Can I love the trees if my desire for wealth
Causes their destruction? I love my mother
Yet hurt her too. It seems that I'm a poor lover.
And how can I love my fellows, wish their health
When I cannot know or love myself?
I don't do what I ought, instead I do the other.
But if I look further into the inner
Mansions, and if I sit in silence and listen,
And if I let the film of familiarity
Be washed, then I receive new sight to see
The world around me anew; it gleams and glistens.
And I am brought to myself, to saint from sinner.

"The Film of Familiarity"

What is this film which obscures and darkens my sight?
How did it come to cover up my eyes?
Why does it darken treasure to a carnival prize
And make a mockery of all that is right
And good and beautiful, holy and bright?
And what has clouded over the enormous size
Of the simplest act? Why don't I rise
In wonder at the brilliance of the night?
It is the film of familiarity,
Habit and custom cataract my vision,
And hang upon my eyes like blinding scales.
I must be cleansed by holy humility--
So that I can overcome this misprision--
But also by art and verse and the telling of tales.

"I Cannot Hear the Stars above"

I cannot hear the stars above,
The ones supposedly moved by Love,
As they turn in celestial course.
Rather I hear myself made hoarse,
Crying defiance to the stars;
My song begins with melancholic bars:
Who can know that they sing
And yet be cold, unfeeling
Knowing we shall never hear,
Never hope, always fear
The coming darkness of the night?
So much do we fear their song
We banish darkness all night long.
Yet the horrid electric hum
Cannot drown the Silent One,
The One who by His silence deafens
The One who moves the seven heavens.

"I Feel Lost in the Darkness of the Night"

I feel lost in the darkness of the night.
The darkest day leads to loss of inner light,
Casting about in the pitch, my eyes
Cast no light on the world around me.
Where is the hope we wait to see?
Where is the treasure, where the pearl of price?
The brutal silence of the heavens deafens.
The violent noise of the world makes no sound.
O Virgin, show us the hidden light of Heaven.
With your glory, Dayspring, the cosmos resounds.

"The Lenses"

I remove my glasses and the solid world grows larger.
The hard lines between the bodies disappear.
Fire more than others shows its nature,
Taking on the yonic shape when She appeared
To a poor man in Guadalupe. I
Cannot focus on any single thing.
Lines and spheres interrupt my expanded sight,
Now here, now there like angels taking wing.
Like Blake, Monet, Van Gogh, I do not see
The world as others do, at least for a moment.
But then the homily ends and I come to be
Normal as glasses remove my impediment.
But do these lenses really correct my sight,
Or without them do I finally see things right?

Autumn

"Autumn is a Jovial Man"

The old man comes in red and tan,
Bringing with him sleep and death,
But Autumn is a jovial man.

He comes festooned with wild plans,
To celebrate before Winter's breath,
The old man comes in red and tan.

Ripened food he stores and cans,
And makes the leaves a harvest wreath
For Autumn is a jovial man.

His bag is filled with roasts and hams
To make up his autumnal feast.
The old man comes in red and tan.

He brings the sleep only he can,
The festive sleep before our death,
For Autumn is a jovial man.

He kills us only to come back again,
The eastern Sun setting in the West.
The old man comes in red and tan.
Old Autumn is a jovial man.

"The Green Man in Autumn"

The air is crisp, the berries have turned brown,
The final harvest has been taken in,
The once new leaves have dropped from the Green Man's crown,
And the Summer's Sun has come to rest and dims.
A cooling breeze sends shivers through his limbs
And fells the apples from their gnarled trees.
In his basket he piles them to the brim
And he makes a draught that fills us up with ease.
He sits in his cave and wanders off in sleep
Taking with him the trees and plants he governs.
The Conifers he sets to watch, to keep
A lonely eye on his domain; for love learns
That what is dead will someday soon arise
And bring with it new life, new joy, new sunrise.

"I Have Seen the Alchemic Eye of the Sun"

I have seen the alchemic eye of the Sun,
Dusty ochre turned to glistering gold.
Its aureate rays all shine and play and run
Across the treetops. The dying light is bold.
Before, the straying clouds hid its power,
But set free, its rays bring life from death,
And we bask in its autumnal hour.
Gilded rays then give way to Autumn's breath.
Crisp air turns cold and the day gives way to night.
The gold and ruby leaves grow dull and fall.
The wandering Moon and twinkling stars cast their light,
And turn the world to silver. My thoughts wander all
Like lonely clouds as I am left to ponder:
What more may come? I wonder, yes, I wonder?

"Smoking a Pipe on a Cool Afternoon"

Like Celtic knots the smoke unfurls and gives
The air an illuminated quality.
Breathed in, blown out, it dies and then it lives.
It gives the room a kind of sublimity.
The cherry heart comes from fire, but air
Keeps the fire alive. A balance must
Be struck. Calm, deliberate, like prayer,
The fire must be fanned. Give in to trust
And let the smoke like incense rise in rings,
In swirls and curls, like Kells now come to life.
And see how like a thurible it sings
Of a world with airish spirits, rife
With things unseen and so unheard of, whole.
All this and more pours from the poet's bole.

"Trees"

There is a microcosm in a tree.
The universe is bound inside a nut.
Instead of stars, her branches are filled with leaves.
Her wandering roots make open ways once shut.
Her bark is home to a million little lives,
Some we can see, but some beyond our sight.
Birds make homes in her branches; They prize
The stable nature of her humble fight.
And in her roots, more creatures make their home.
A fungal network taught them all to talk,
And helps them send some food right through the loam.
A hidden world exists from stem to stalk,
And yet this is not all there is to see.
This is not all that makes a tree a tree.

"From Star to Star"

From star to star the reflected light pours down,
Filling my heart, my soul, with light from the
Cosmos. The heavens make their home in me.
The Glory of the Lord declares angelic
Voices as the macrocosm becomes microcosmic.
The eternal Love that moves the stars comes down
And joins me to eternity. Yet the
ordinary makes it hard to see.
But eternal Love now beats desire erotic,
Agapeic; microcosm becomes macrocosmic.

"Daimoniocene"

Fungiluminescence lights their hallowed
Halls. The winds inside the earth give them
Air, with ancient hearths in ancient dens.
They followed wending rivers down, they followed
The River Alph and by its mouth were swallowed.
Industrial fires devoured their homes, their glens,
And made the upper world too small for them.
So they burrowed under barrows and hollowed
Out the earth to make themselves a home.
Fungal fronds connect them all to trees,
Connect them to the earth above unseen.
We hope to see them rise up through the loam,
Like man-sized moles, majestic majesties,
When Anthropocene becomes Daimoniocene.

"Thomas the Rhymer Comes Home"

I looked down that bonnie road
      And on it did I tread.
It often seemed the road of life,
      But sometimes of the dead.

Marvels were there on that road
      I could not tell them all.
Gnomes and dwarves, elves and fay;
      Dragons fly and giants fall.

More wondrous still, the trees I saw,
      The mountains rising greater,
The sun, the moon, the dancing planets,
      And man in our enchanted nature.

I found myself on the Faërie Road
      And onward did we tread.
We entered home by the forest door,
      And found the wine and bread.

Winter

"Winter Breathes Me into Life"

She carves the old out with a knife,
But just as I'm about to die,
Winter breathes me into life.

Winter wears a crown, one rife
With thorns, with thorns and leaves of holly.
She carves the old out with a knife.

She is Evening's loving wife,
And gives to us the clearest sky.
Winter breathes me into life.

Life with her is often strife,
But one we cannot simply pass by.
She carves the old out with a knife.

She gives to us our one belief,
That the Sun has not yet died.
Winter breathes me into life.

And so she comes with harp and fife
To bring an end to Satan's lie.
She carves the old out with a knife,
Dear Winter, breathe me into life.

"Yule Log"

Found amongst the garden bracken
        I bring you in to heat my home,
But more than this is bound to happen
        When the Yule Log is begun.

Tradition from our pagan past?
        Or antiquarian imagination?
Doesn't matter if the Yule Log lasts
        In its immolation.

Its smoke like prayer and incense rises
        To God above, alone.
I ask for heavenly surprises,
        For God to bless my home.

Giving back what I have found,
        Receiving warmth and pleasure,
I pray to live on sacred ground
        And filled with sacred treasure.

Burn slow, not quick, upon my hearth;
        Don't yield yourself just yet.
For through you God gives a kind of new life
        And I am nearly dead.

"The Ballad of Whisky"

You warm me from the inside out
      And fill me to the brim.
You charm me with your Scottish clout,
      With your amber color dim.

Now stoke the fire and pack your pipe,
      Fill your glasses well.
Your drink is not of common type,
      Please listen to it tell

Of island home and salt sea air,
      Of peat and smoke and fire;
Of mounts and woods and old men's prayer,
      Of Andrew's cross and English ire.

It sings the songs of Scotland
      With every single sip,
It sends me to my homeland
      When it meets my lips.

"Greening the Church"

We bring into the church the evergreen,
Fresh boughs of trees that last all winter long.
And as we place them round, we sing a song
About peace on earth, goodwill to men.
We set them up to decorate, it seems,
To bring some festive Christmas cheer along.
The boughs remind us of the ancient Yule log
Our ancestors once burned for the year's end.
But more is happening than might appear.
We bring the Green Man into the Church,
And not in stone, but in the trees themselves,
To Winter with us at the end of the year,
To bring with him not just pines, but elm and birch.
Creation comes to see the baby the dwell.

"Blood Moon"

The silent planet passes through the love
That's shared by Sun and Moon. Their love is light,
And we cast a pall on our neighbor from above.
Her face made red by intercepted light
Scattered through the ethereal breath of the gods.
Blood moon they call it, but whose is the blood?
Is it ours? Is it the blood of man who trods
Upon the earth but a little while, good
For little and evil for much? Or does the Sun bleed,
And his blood is shed upon his sister the Moon?
Or does the Moon bleed as the oceans' tides she feeds?
It is all these. For Christ who bled will soon
Come again, the one foretold by the Sky,
The one who lives, the Light who had to die.

"The Bells of Elfland"

Snow falls softly on this New Year's Eve.
The radiant Sun shines boldly New Year's Day;
And I am here, listening, ready to take my leave,
To say goodbye, to meander on my way.
For I hear the bells and trumpets who
Call unto my soul, the bells of Elfland
Redound in my heart and subtly lead me through
Onto the Straight Road that leads to life, to wealth and
Peril. Yet I do not go. Another call
Brings me back to myself. A child's laugh,
My wife's smile, they are to me my all.
The bells of Elfland give way to Church, my wrath,
My passion, my wanderlust they bring to an end.
In gratefulness for Change I bow, my knees I bend.

"Murmuration"

Twisting and swirling in amoebic shape,
The citizens of the sky take their strange flight,
Gyring and gimboling, a heavenly wave,
A living, breathing Mobius Strip on high.
Starlings, why do you dance in this shimmering form,
Combining and recombining, phase to phase,
Transitioning like water to ice, then warmed
To vapor through sublimating ways?
Perhaps it is just physics and survival.
You do not dance, but fight to stay alive.
Your ratio of one to seven is primal
Physics, causing you to turn and jump and dive.
But something tells me there is more to see,
If only we had hearts and eyes set free.

"The Quality of Light Passing through Ice"

All your rays gleam upon the snow,
And turn it into a many-jewelled land.
Clouds appear as the wind begins to blow
But you will not die, no you will take your stand
And shine across the gleaming land so bright.
The snow begins to feel your distant warmth
And in your blaze I am bereft of sight,
So I cannot see the icy crystals form.
But when my sight returns, I see them there,
Piercing toward the ground like cruel claws.
But in your light they take a different air,
And look now more like crystals, and give me pause
To look not only once, but to look twice
At the quality of light passing through ice.

Spring

"But Spring Will Come Like a Thief in the Night"

The days grow long, but Winter's wind still bites,
And every morning grass is covered in frost,
But Spring will come like a thief in the night.

Her greening power will make everything right.
She will bring home all things that once were lost,
As the days grow long, and Winter's wind still bites.

We may not yet see her, for sin has dimmed our sight,
And in her tempests all our senses tossed,
But Spring will come like a thief in the night.

Her verdant power does not rest alone in might,
But in meekness that knows to count the cost,
As the days grow long and Winter's wind still bites.

Plants will bud and birds will take new flight,
Like new-learned words only just recently glossed,
For Spring will come like a thief in the night.

Yes, she will come, we have no need of fright,
For Death's domain has been emptied out and tossed.
Yes, the days grow long, and Winter's wind still bites,
But Spring will come like a thief in the night.

"The Green Man in Spring"

His leafy crown grows golden buds as Rain
Begins to fill her forest lover's heart.
The weather warms and cools again and again,
Just as his heart is warmed and cooled in part.
When warming up, he reaches out his tendrils,
Digging deep and waking all the trees,
But in the cool, he sleeps and dreams of petals
Blossoming and falling into the sea.
And through the Sun, he sends his greening power
Into elm and oak and maple, rowan, birch.
He makes them pregnant at the proper hour,
Yet he cannot be found, no matter how hard we search.
He's the Green Man, and he was once our friend,
And we may yet know him, before the final end.

"Väinämöinen"

Väinämöinen sang,
The waters listened.
Spirit of Arable
Made the trees grow.
Väinämöinen cleared
The land for man,
But man then cleared
The land
Of Väinämöinen.

"At the Root of the World there Is a Tree"

At the root of the world there is a tree,
Not a tree but the world tree, Ygdrasil.
In its branches are the stars, wandering gods
Light its leaves, which it eats and radiates.
In its deep roots all stories find their germ.
They shoot up one here, another there, none
Whole until at last they meet in the trunk,
Joined together illuminating and
Illuminated each by each. The leaves
Effoliating stories now combined;
Recombined shedding and receiving light.
At the root of the world there is a tree,
Not a tree but the world tree, Ygdrasil.

"Spring comes to New Hampshire"

The melting snow leaves the ground soft,
Readying the land for planting.
Trees are drained and sugar shacks are stuffed
To the brim, boiling, grunting
Old and young alike delight.
But promised warmth always leaves us wanting
As frost is found in early morning light.
Yet the cold of Winter cannot stay,
It soon gives way to mornings warm and bright.
After death comes life, some say,
Always returning, never quite the same.
The long nights passed by longer days,
Winter's sleep becomes vernal fame.
And I too find myself changed;
Like a star I feel my life aflame.
The fire burns, I am not pained,
But refined and iridescent shine.
My death in sleep is thus exchanged
For this greening life of mine.
As herbs grow so too do I, breathed
Into life like prayer at Compline,
Like effoliation, trees leaved,
Budding first then bursting forth
In peace, like a sword sheathed.
This Spring will see a fulsome dearth
Of life to live that is of worth.

"The Boston Public Gardens"

The greening power of the grass and trees
Cannot keep out the sounds of city-life.
No birdsong can overcome, no bees
Can hum loud enough to silence all the strife.
And lovely petals fall while sirens resound,
Cars constantly intruding with combusted
Noise; the sky filled with the flapping sound
Of helicopters flying overhead.
And yet, for a moment the cacophony is gone,
And I hear the water ripple, the sparrow sing;
The wind makes music through the branches, a song
I once half-heard when I was a little thing.
It may be that this music is an illusion,
But still I'll gladly wait for its conclusion.

"Sleeping Giants"

The fog is laid like blankets on the old
And sleeping giants. They were here before us,
Rising slowly out of the ground, bold
And tall in youth, now old and slumberous.
They sleep and lie in wait, perhaps they dream
Of days gone by, before the wind and rain
Beat them down like wizened men and women.
Or perhaps they dream of when they'll rise again.
Whatever these sleeping giants dream, they wait,
They wait for the return of the Lord of the Forest.
When he returns they will at last awake,
Though they may rise before just for a moment.
And when, in the end, the trees will clap their hands,
The Mountains will sing for joy in all the lands.

"The Word Wood, or the Library Forest"

There are words in the wood, on every single branch,
Reaching out their arms to touch the sky.
They do not break and they will never blanch,
But they'll keep trying, o yes, o yes, they'll try
To reach us, to teach us, to find us and bring us in
To the dappled places, the darkened places
Below the earth, below the mushrooms grim
And down, and down to infinite root-filled spaces
Where we'll be captured, raptured into tree veins
And feed the ones who feed us with their breath.
We'll give up ourselves, the last of our remains
And breath the treeish words of life and death.
We hear the words bound up in forest wood;
We can become them; it will do us good.

Summer

"Summer Sings His Halcyon Song"

The Sun grows hot and the days grow long
as the days are filled with wondrous light,
As Summer sings his halcyon song.

All is well, there is no more wrong,
For the old ills have been set to rights,
As the Sun grows hot and the days grow long.

Summer makes us all belong
To his Kingdom of the Summer Sunlight,
As he sings his halcyon song.

He strikes upon the festal gong,
And gives up ruling by his might,
As the Sun grows hot and the days grow long.

He says that he will not prolong
Our waiting anymore this night,
As he sings his halcyon song.

For the peace for which we long,
He gives it up without a fight,
As the Sun grows hot and the days grow long,
And Summer sings his halcyon song.

"The Green Man"

Effoliating foliage, he haunts
His local habitation. The tutelary
Spirit, ripener of wildest blackberry,
Protector of the bees' humblest wants.
From cloves to honeysuckles, from elm to maple,
He cares for the wood as if it were his garden.
The iridescent lights of night are starred in
His eyes. He gathers food for his greenwood table.
And once, in ages now so long forgotten,
His greening power helped even us to grow.
He was our teacher and our dearest friend.
But now on the New Wine we are besotted,
Drunk on this technological flow.
Still, even in the gales he will not bend.

"To the TBF"

We gather round the wooden table, all
Ready to uncover the mysteries divine.
These holy mysteries on which we dine
Are our food. The inn provides our glasses, tall
For beer or cider, but for whiskey, small.
Pipes lovingly, liturgically incline
Us to our topics for the day. We shine
With smiles, with eyes made bright by light eternal.
But the bells and bustle call us back to life.
We pack our things, prepare ourselves to leave,
Our holy pipes expire, our glasses empty,
And we return to home, to love, to strife.
For none can live in aether lest they cleave
To air under the stars, to air sublunary.

"Hiking the Winant Trails with My Sons"

Dark and close and bright and open,
We travel from one world to another.
Lighted faces give light to the den
Of birds and bugs, deer and others.
We see their secret, nightly work,
The capped mushrooms now cropping up,
The moss-covered stones who do not shirk
Their duties until the sun comes up.
The messages of trees sent by web,
Woven of fungal fronds, run root
To bow; the brook courses only to ebb
As we travelers pass the mute
Genius of the forest, silenced
By the fierce electric hum
Of power lines placed in violence.
And yet, perhaps, he still may come.
Perhaps what has been silenced can
Be brought to sound again, and we
Can beckon from his exile, the Green Man
To live, as he ought, amongst us. You see,
He disappeared into folk legend.
The way once shut, must be opened.

"I Want to Hear the Trees Again"

When Alfred stood upon the shore,
He saw the waves come crashing over
The rocks of Ancient Albion.

A boat was riding on the waves
To take him through forgotten caves
Beyond the Sea to fair Elfland.

The ship was silver as the moon.
"The time to leave is now or soon
Your way to Faërie will be lost."

So said the fair Elf-Queen.
Would he dare the Perilous Realm?
Or would he stay on safer shores?

He quickly climbed into the boat,
Ready to sail, ready to float
Through courses strange to Elvenhome.

Too soon, it seemed, the voyage done
And Alfred walked about as one
Enchanted by the elven folk.

Through forests first the Elf-Queen led
Where leaves were of bright gold and red,
Where rustlings sounded harmony.

And then past pools young Alfred walked
Through meres as man and elf did talk
Of mortal and immortal joys.

At last they reached the elven keep
And there the King began to weep
And asked of Alfred why he came.

"What do you come to take away,
What beauty will you not let stay
In its fair and native land?"

"My King," young Alfred said to him,
"I would not cause this place to dim;
I want to hear the trees again."

"Oceanus"

Why do the Ocean's waves keep rolling in
Smoothing all that's rough with their rough force?
I wish these waves could smooth away my sin
And turn into a stallion my lustful horse.
The music of the spheres causes ebb and flow
And raises the sublime on briny air.
Masculine strength gives way to beauty's glow,
And I am left to wonder who is there?
What genius of the rocks and beaches guides me?
Why does my spirit seem so often to roam
In sin and in the longing for the sea?
The answer's somewhere in that celestial song
And over the sea to where I will belong.

"This Plum Tree Bower, My Haven"

Beneath this plum tree bower, my haven,
I sit and watch the world spin on.
Round it spins like a whirligig,
Never stopping, always dancing.
And this ever constant revolution,
Always spinning just the same,
Causes terrestrial commotion
From day to night and night to day,
From Autumn's harvest to Winter's death,
To Spring's rebirth and Summer's sun.
I see it in the fruiting plums
Dangling just above my head.
For now they're green and small and round
Like tiny planets hanging from the World Tree,
But soon they'll grow and turn to cosmic
Ellipse, and red like blood their juice
Will run, when I taste my first bite from the harvest.

"Lammas"

The Summer Sun has burned the crop of wheat.
The ears of corn have ripened on the stalk.
We pick and grind them to make a treat
Formed from the four elements; yet we balk:
How can air and earth and water and fire
Come to form this alchemical loaf?
What is it in this world that it so transpires
That the basest elements become both
Simple and complex, an ordinary
Marvel, a whole more than the sum of its parts?
What spirits hide in the air extraordinary
That raise this lowly dough into an art?
This is the staff of life formed from the dead,
The living magic, the simple loaf of bread.

Saints and Other Songs of the Church

"St. Hildegard"

O holy abbess, keeper of the garden,
You learned to read the blessed book of nature.
You saw behind the veil of habit and custom
And through to the greening power of earth, holy verdure.
You worked with planets and birds and animals and stones,
Knowing when their ministrations would heal.
You read the earth, right to its very bones,
But you knew the works of heaven just as well.
God used the wondrous cosmos to show you how
The book of revelation might be read.
He showed you heavenly choirs who before him bow
And took you on the path we all must tread.
And so, St. Hildegard, please say a prayer
That we may one day meet you in heavenly air.

"The Saints and the Stag"

A pagan hunts the hart deep in the wood,
Following his chestnut enemy.
The stag, looking for his love and for food,
Leads the man away from his family.
It is a merry chase that ends in death,
As the deer is hunted for glory and for fame.
But then the unexpected takes his breath
As the hunters sees a light shine from his game.
A crucifix and voice soon appear
Between the stately stag's enormous antlers.
God used the noble nature of the deer
To prove himself the Lord, the One, the Granter
Of Eternal Glory and of Fame
Through eternal life and through his name.

"The Statue and the Woman"

Before me stands a statue of the Virgin Mary.
This poor Jewish girl's skin is lily white.
Her robes ornate, she stabs the snake and carries
Porcelain perfect Jesus as though he's light.
They are perfect, no blemish anywhere.
Mary stands upon her pedestal,
She stands immaculate and stares
Out upon the congregation, whole.
But to my left, a crumpled woman sits,
Her body ravaged by genetic disease.
She talks of early anger and her fits
Of rage, of wanting life to be different, please!
But now she loves her broken gift from God,
For God broke his body too, his spoken Word.

"St. Brigid"

Give to me your prayers, o blessed Bride,
O woman of Kildare, please bring me home.
Show me Christ and drench me to the bone
With your love for him, the love in which you died.
You give the Church of Oak a source of pride
For there, through you, God's grace miraculously shone.
Your prayers were said to cause the rains to run,
And you blessed the babes who in broken families cried.
Yet who are you really, Brigid of Kildare?
Were you a pagan goddess, as some believe,
Worshipped at the Imbolc, the start of Spring?
Or are you the patron saint of poets and brewers,
An abbess of Christ under the oaken leaves?
I believe you're with the angels, and you sing.

"St. David"

Dewi o Cymru, poetry's patron,
We anglicized your name and called you David.
You spread in Wales the knowledge of salvation,
Yet you cared for creatures too, you were not craven,
Thinking all things existed just for our use.
You gave us bread and beer and cheese to feed
The poor, so God's creatures would not be abused.
You preached the Truth and set the sinners free.
And now, my namesake, I ask you for your prayers.
You and I are poets like the king
Who came before us. Please help me sing new airs
And with beloved David reach out and bring
Me to new heights that I may see
Through eyes like yours, may see reality.

"St. Patrick"

In dreams you heard your mournful captors' cry,
Calling you to be Christ where you once suffered.
Your heart was opened for them, it was not buffered,
But porous, taking them and leading them high
Above and beyond their druidical sense of the sky
As your paschal fire flames rose up unshuttered.
You showed them a hidden God with face uncovered,
And taught them three-in-one was not a lie.
You bound upon your breastplate a world connected,
And like the druids, you saw everything together.
For trees and rocks and air are bound up with us,
And seraphim and saints show us God reflected.
You saw the Spirit in the wind that blows a feather,
You showed us Christ above, before, and in us.

"St. Kevin"

You knelt inside your hermit's cell to pray,
Reciting psalms and worshipping your God.
Your narrow little cell was all you had,
And so one hand was stretched out into the day.
And while you sang your psalms, a bird came to lay
Her eggs in a nest made of your outstretched hand.
She chose you for your safety, your closeness to God,
Or perhaps like Mary, she needed any place to stay.
But why is this a story that we tell?
Why write about a crazy old man, alone
In the wild, singing under a waterfall,
Or having an otter return his book which fell?
Perhaps we do it to remind us that our home
Is shared with people, angels, beasts, with all.

"St. Francis"

"Rebuild my church," were the words you heard that day.
They rang throughout your young, Italian ears.
Then you came down with a case of holy tears,
Believing it was your family's job to pay
To rebuild a fallen chapel where it lay
Alone, unused, suffused with earthly fear.
Your father brought you to court, which made you tear
The very clothes from your back and walk away.
And so, you went among the twittering birds,
Making Lady Poverty your loving wife.
You preached to all God's creatures whom you met,
And saw the Gospel was more than just mere words.
This made you give the Word every ounce of your life,
Thus you built up the Church to be holy and Cosmic.

"St. Columba and the Loch Ness Monster"

You sent young Luigne to entice the beast,
And he went without a moment's hesitation.
He swam into the river's fluctuation.
All who watched thought you sent him to be a feast.
The hungry serpent swam and roared and reached
The swimming boy with hungry salutation.
All those who looked on watched in fear and frustration,
As you, Columba, looked on in holy peace.
For you knew how to read the book of creation,
What songs or signs would send the creature running.
By the grace of God and by the Holy Rood,
You sent the creature to its new habitation.
Pictish heathens stood, their minds all wondering,
"Who is this Christ we may have misunderstood?"

"Burning a Fire on the Feast of St. Lucy"

What is light? The waves and particles?
The radiation warming and giving sight?
The Sun? The stars? The fire lit at night
Reduced at last to embers, burning coals?
The flip of a switch, vibrations electrical?
The soft blue glow of our phones, outshining sunlight
And starlight and moonlight and firelight and all the lights
From the birth of the Cosmos, reflecting, residual?
O Lucy, o iridescent one, please speak,
Please tell us how it is that you still shine
When all the lights we know cannot reach you?
What is the source of your celestial hue?
And how far beyond the Universe must I climb
To reach your home, the holy mountain's peak?

"St. Cecilia"

You wear the virgin's crown and martyr's too.
You heard the silent music of the heaven's sing
Inside your holy, Christian's heart; and through
Your virgin-voice you converted many, preaching
The gospel of the unseen now made clear.
You helped your husband see reality
When he washed away the lens of sin and fear.
Then he watched your angel consort crown your beauty.
You shined with virgin's light and then the martyr's,
As the tyrants tried to smother and behead.
You sang of Christ, you sang and did not falter,
You sang of Christ as your veil with blood turned red.
You closed your eyes and made your name come true,
Now pray for us as we now turn to you.

"The Annunciation"

"Let it be as you have said," the Handmaid
Of the Lord gives her consent. Her *Fiat*
Echoes back to when God eternally brought
The stars, the earth and all that was ever made
Into its bright existence. Through what she said
Mary becomes a kind––though humanly not
Divinely––of co-creatrix; it is her lot
To be the Mother of our Lord and his handmaid.
But we should not forget that Heaven's Queen
Was a young and humble Jewish girl.
She lived and loved and laughed and had her fears.
She walked the streets of Palestine, seen
And heard and likely suffered insults hurled
At her. This is our Queen, who cried real tears.

"St. Joseph"

In the moonlit night he leads them on,
The Holy Mother and her still young child.
He knows that he may lead them to the wild
And lonely places of the world. "Be gone,"
The Angel said, and so before the dawn
They left. Perhaps the infant Jesus smiled
And cooed and laughed as the Moon and stars compiled
Their holy song. Perhaps the ocean was calm.
But Rachel wailed and weeped for children lost,
And Herod, like our sin, raged on, and Death
Seemed to hold all in its sway. The Fall
Remained in place. But Egypt leads to the Cross,
To rocks and stones that call out without breath.
But while they walk the stars sound their silent call.

"Our Lady of Sorrows"

Your heart was pierced by seven sorrowful swords,
And now you wear the black veil of one mourning.
You speak the roses red, but not with words,
But with the bleeding of your heart, now warming
From sadness into joy, for in three days
The mysteries you treasured in your heart
Will cast the paint out with a holy blaze
Of Light, of Fire that burns in you our hearth.
And like the blessed moon which mediates
The rays of light cast on it from the sun,
So you immaculate will conflagrate
And burn with fire from your resurrected Son.
And so we turn to you when we're in need,
Our Lady of Sorrows, our Heaven's Holy Queen.

"The Light of Christ"

His precious blood poured down with water and light.
The Light of all the world for us was snuffed out.
Just as a candle standing in the night
Is finally hushed, leaving darkness and doubt,
So he too was hushed, uttering his final
Cry. But Death's domain could not contain
Him. He swallowed death which tried to swallow
Him. To give us life is why he came.
And now this light shines through the wine and bread,
And we're consumed by what we're meant to eat.
For he consumes all things, from life to death,
And brings us through and to our final feast.
For now he feeds us with his bread and wine,
But on that day, it's Light on which we'll dine.

"Transfiguration"

Taboric light, shekinah mist unveils
The Truth, the hidden Light behind the Shadow.
The dull becomes radiant, and holy blows
The Wind. The three men continue to tell their tale.
Moses and Elijah prep the Holy Grail.
Peter sees and kneels and bends and bows
While James and John sit silent, Peter knows
Not what to say, his understanding fails.
The Light and mist return from whence they come,
Only to find their way back to the earth.
For Christ and Spirit dwell inside us all,
And he united all things from our home
To his unapproachable divinity, our worth
Refreshed with light and life from one eternal.

"Christ the King"

We crowned you first as king with bloody holly,
The droplets of your blood, they stained the berries.
Next we drove you on bearing our folly,
And jeered not knowing it was our sin you carried.
We nailed your hands to the beam, your arms outstretched,
And nailed your feet to form the Greek letter *tau*.
We raised you up as one unloved and wretched,
And yet you seek to forgive us anyhow.
Then we pierced your side to make you bleed,
And holy blood and water came raining down,
But with this blood and flesh you wish to feed
Us. You made the Holy Grail out of the ground.
By your five wounds we are washed and clean,
To be more human than we've ever been.

"The Holy Grail"

Who held the holy Chalice that caught his blood
Blended with the shimmering Water of Life,
Catching it, this strange admixture rife
With all the active potency of the Good?
And who was washed in this outpouring flood,
Made into the Bridegroom's new found wife,
Washed away from pain, from death, from strife
And into the paradisal garden wood?
It was the Earth who received the Blood and Water,
And the Green Man carried it through the flowers,
The trees, through all living things without fail.
He bore the Chalice he became to the Altar;
Christ spreading through everything by his greening power,
And so the Earth became the Holy Grail.

Printed in the USA
CPSIA information can be obtained
at www.ICGtesting.com
LVHW011910170823
755570LV00003B/8